JEFFREY BILHUBER
EVERYDAY DECORATING

JEFFREY BILHUBER
EVERYDAY DECORATING

WRITTEN WITH JACQUELINE TERREBONNE

RIZZOLI
NEW YORK

New York Paris · London Milan

INTRODUCTION

Let's face it—we're in an age of Instagram inspiration. And you know what? I'm absolutely loving it. I'm a big believer in posting, liking, DM-ing, and everything that comes with it. But there are so many awe-inspiring, jaw-dropping design images out there, it's hard to know what to do with this total information overload. Seeing a pretty room is one thing, but knowing how to distill what makes that space work and translate those takeaways into your own home is an entirely different matter. For that you really need an expert, and that's where I come in.

In **EVERYDAY DECORATING**, my fifth book, I've broken down exactly what makes diverse spaces invite us in, and why they remain alluring. Whether the photos were snapped weeks before we went to press or twenty years ago, each of these rooms has made a mark, and I'm going to tell you why with practical advice and easy-to-follow tips that inspire and empower you to make enlightened design decisions. Never again will you sit in the middle of a room asking, "How come I have all this nice stuff and I'm still unhappy?" or "Why doesn't it go together?"

Those questions and more will be answered in snapshots that point you in the right direction—and to make things super clear, I will tell you the answers. Who can argue with that? None of this information will go out of style or feel dated, because every tip is based on the foundations of great decorating.

To keep us on task, I decided to break this book into different chapters that illustrate the universal goals of every home, no matter where it's located or what the budget. They are the words I hear over and over from clients again and again, so I've dedicated a chapter to each one of these eight essential signifiers: comfortable, happy, colorful, personal, lighter and brighter, sexy, charming, and cozy.

Ultimately, I hope when you look at each page you'll be able to say, "Well, I never thought of it like that." That's how the message will stick with you the next time you're shopping for a sofa, making a bed, or considering paint colors. I'm not going to lie—this advice isn't only for you. I've given the same nuggets of design gold to my clients like Anna Wintour, Iman and the late David Bowie, Mariska Hargitay, and Elsa Peretti. I didn't hold anything back with them, and I won't with you either.

COMFORTAB[LE]

Comfort is the biggest driver in every one of my projects. No matter how many client presentations I've made about color, form, or texture, invariably the conversation always circles back to comfort. Of course, I can pick a chair of exquisite provenance and sublime beauty, but at the end of the day you're going to want to sit in it and feel relaxed and at ease.

Listen, there's not enough space in most homes to set aside a showpiece room. Instead you want to create rooms that put you at ease even when you're wowed by their beauty. Have you ever wanted to just stay in a room forever? That's exactly what comfort does. So, take charge and make sure there are more than a couple of comfortable rooms in a home and that every room achieves this goal. Look outside as well for creating thoughtful spaces that make you want to linger alfresco when the weather is right. There is valuable real estate all around you, and unlocking its potential is our goal.

Much of bringing comfort to a room is based on certain classical traditional proportions that have merit. I'm a big believer in the comfort of the familiar—this idea that if we're concerned with making the wrong decision we will default to what we know. These subconscious notions of where things should go based on what we've been surrounded by in the past are the perfect jumping-off point. They're easy to put into practice and work no matter how modern your personal style. Once you've established a good plan, you can pick furniture designed to address the needs of the room, because comfort comes in all shapes and sizes.

You're not done when you've picked the perfect chair. That sense of comfort needs to carry through once you've taken a seat. Is there a reading lamp casting enough light but not too much? Is there a place to put a glass down within arm's reach? If someone comes into the room, do you see them enter or do they startle you from behind?

Comfort is more than foam and feathers. This feeling comes from marrying all the right forms and functions—when everything falls into place, there are no questions of why something is there or what its purpose is. And there are certainly design elements that are hallmarks of comfort: the intimacy of a fireplace, the ease of an ottoman, the warmth of a canopy bed. So throw away the idea that comfort is just a bunch of throw pillows and discover how I create a room that embraces you.

Of course you need one comfortable sofa in a living room.

But that doesn't mean every other piece needs to be stuffed, plumped, and squished. Furniture in frame provides the perfect contrast, as its sculptural form plays off the weight and mass of the larger piece. Although it might not be the first place you choose to sit, such seating presents the opportunity to sit face to face with someone and have a real conversation.

Someone needs to invent a modern word for sectional sofa.

But it should not be something that brings to mind tragic '80s modular furniture. This chic design commands the entire room while creating enough lounging space for everyone to pile on. The lively, exotic pattern actually disguises the bulk of this massive piece, as do the pillows, which I recommend in patterned pairs with no fewer than three in each corner.

COMFORTABLE

COMFORTABLE

No one is going to say no to an ottoman, especially when you can use one just about anywhere. This workhorse can be a chair, a table, a footrest, a dog bed. Beyond that, done up in a statement fabric or embellished with unexpected trim, this piece gives a room the touch of personality it needs.

For your big
entrance,
please don't
make the
mistake
of statement
wallpaper.

It's overplayed and
overshadows what's to come.
Why not paint the ceiling a
dazzling poison green lacquer?
Now there's something your
guests won't forget. And now
the walls can become the
perfect neutral backdrop for
works of art that tell the
story of the person who lives
there, instead of broadcasting
a generic pattern.

A decorated entry hall is the most welcoming of invitations.

I'm not talking about the stereotypical console and a pair of stiff chairs that have never been used. A fully furnished entry creates a sense of arrival, especially with exquisite pieces like an over-scaled Hudson Valley mirror hovering over a diminutive bedroom-size Louis XVI mantel that take advantage of a space that often goes to waste.

COMFORTABLE

COMFORTABLE

Ever heard of a chofa?

Neither a chair nor a sofa, this glorious piece of furniture is just right in front of a fireplace, where it provides the perfect spot to snuggle for one or more. I match a pair of chofas with a square ottoman the same width. Soon, the whole family will be curled up in front of the flickering flames.

Most decorators start a furniture plan with the largest flat wall, but when there's a fireplace in play, I start right there.

Everyone wants to cozy up to a fire, and many a great evening start and finish right there. A pair of chairs facing each other, with an ottoman in between, invite you to sink in, kick up your feet, and jump-start the conversation.

When it comes to chairs, I like to exercise a variety of arm shapes to maximize seating options.

A rolled arm on the sofa provides just enough space to take a temporary perch. The saddle-arm sculpted frame doesn't take up too much space while creating a seat of power. An armless slipper chair, scaled up for use in the living room, is easy to slide in and out of—perfect for the host or hostess on duty. After all, comfort comes in all shapes and sizes.

COMFORTABLE

English rooms tend
to be filled with
furniture, but an
American family
living in an English
house brings edited
clarity and comfort.
The primary goal of upholstery is
comfort, so proportions should be a direct
response to who is going to sit in the
furniture and what the purpose will be.

COMFORTABLE

There's already plenty of wood in a dining room, with the polished table always taking center stage.

So many people worry that upholstered chairs will be difficult to clean, but there are other options for creating comfort. These modernist chairs with leather seats are a cinch to clean, while a contrasting fabric on the back enhances and loosens up what can be the stiffest room in a house.

Nothing is friendlier than a round table.

Breakfast rooms are busy places with family members going about their schedules, and a round table helps to circulate all that traffic. It invites conversation, which this space did not foster at first: the Moroccan tile floor echoed with the sound of dragging chair legs and clanking forks. A simple fix was putting down a few area rugs, so you can actually hear when someone asks you to pass the sugar.

COMFORTABLE

COMFORTABLE

Nothing is more unsettling than being adrift in a big or even a not-so-big room.

A small, low folding screen corrects the problem by carving up the plot into cozier groupings, while still allowing the eye to take in the space as a whole. The primary objective of any seating plan is for the room and its occupants to envelop you. The screen, a much undervalued piece of furniture, creates a wraparound effect that helps the eye focus.

This sleeping porch is a snoozer's delight.

One fifteen-foot black wicker sofa, outfitted with two twin mattresses end to end, commands the entire space. With such a statement piece, the rest of the furniture can be dialed back—like these small chairs that only amplify the magnitude of the room's star. Don't skimp on the pillows though. Piling them on in as many patterns and colors as possible will only invite more lounging.

The most common instinct is to push a sofa up against a wall, but one of my hallmarks is back-to-back sofas.

There's always a dilemma about which direction to face. Should it be the fireplace or the view, the television or the fireplace? This way you can have your cake and eat it too. It's the perfect solution in rooms that are too long, and it breaks up conversations from the sprawl of one big seating group.

COMFORTABLE

A reminder that a window seat actually faces into a room, not toward the view.

That said, be sure to add a chair or two (or four!) that incorporate the occupants so they can have a conversation. If your space is limited, try an ottoman in front of the window seat, which can achieve the same goal.

Don't resign yourself to thinking that comfortable means heaps of pillows or chairs so plush you can't get out of them.

A tight, fitted seat can be just as welcoming, especially when it's deep enough that you can curl up your feet in it. Think about the depth of a seat cushion when you shop for a chair and bring your damn tape measure to the store. Or at least ask the question, "What's the inside seat depth of this chair?" Here's the scoop: industry standard suggests that twenty-one-and-a-half inches is what consumers really want. That's great if you want to be seated at an upholstered bus stop! In our New York City workrooms we consider a twenty-seven-inch seat depth the height of luxury. Now you've got the acceptable range, your tape measure, and the answer to your questions. Let's go shopping!

COMFORTABLE

Linear forms are the antithesis of comfort.

To give this swanky pied-à-terre a more inviting feel, I repeated the idea of rounded forms wherever possible. From the midcentury coffee table to the nineteenth-century barrel-back chairs, curves abound. Even on the floor, we skipped the standard rectangular rugs for more organically shaped steer hides to lend a more relaxed air.

COMFORTABLE

Everyone's a winner when you add a games table to a family room.

The thirty-nine-inch square table is the workhorse piece you won't believe you lived without. Of course, it's perfect for puzzles and a hand of Gin Rummy, but it also suggests a good lunch on a lazy day or coffee, croissants, and a newspaper for one, especially when paired with generous chairs set on casters.

I don't shy away from much, especially decorative pillows.

Twenty years ago, bed linens were all hidden under a bedspread. Now that they take center stage, it's important not to overlook the usefulness and personality added by a mix of fabrics and cushions. You should dress a bed just as you would a sofa, and take advantage of all the wonderful patterns and sizes out there.

You can't go wrong if you default to something you love, and better yet, it will never go out of style.

Decorating with elements filled with history and meaning (such as this map that has been in my family for generations) will connect you to your house and instantly create rooms with the comfort of the familiar.

COMFORTABLE

COMFORTABLE

You'll sleep better if you have a practical bedside table.

Rounded or chamfered edges are a good place to start as they eliminate those sharp edges that torment you at night. A waterproof top, such as glass, goes a long way when you need to set a bottle of water down in the middle of the night, and a shelf or moveable tray creates extra space for books and devices.

There's just as much opportunity to create comfort on the outside of the house as there is on the inside.

A beautiful outdoor room comes together with a matched set of furniture that is layered with humble elements in straw and rattan. Then, anchor the space with a simple straw mat on the floor and channel your inner Gatsby with weather-treated curtains to catch the breeze and filter the light.

COMFORTABLE

HAPPY

Happy doesn't begin and end with sunny yellow rooms. You can find it in so many places: an explosion of pattern, a crisp all-white bed, a surprising glossy orange ceiling. Once there's a joyful component in a room, it becomes contagious and the whole space just wants to sing.

As a decorator, I'm happiest when I see a room that's used, loved, and enjoyed. When I go back to a project and it's apparent that a space has been inhabited and the clients have added personal mementos, my heart just soars. Real stories have unfolded there, and people have wanted to stay and linger because they feel good there. At the beginning of the process, clients often identify things that make them sad in their homes, and it's my job to fix that and create a backdrop that enlivens their moods and brings delight every day.

To achieve this, there are happy colors and patterns that won't steer you wrong. Gingham springs to mind, along with the unflappable appeal of blue with white. But most of the time, happiness is not scripted. It truly is the element you didn't see coming that brings a smile to someone's face, and I try to fill each room with as many of these elements as possible. Too many rooms are vacuous and empty. People want to believe that having something sleek and clean will yield happiness, but ultimately you can't settle into these hollow shells.

Define your key goals, and then be fearless in your execution of it. When we are liberated and confident in the way we approach our rooms, we yield a happier result, especially when it's mixed with spontaneity and optimism. So, go the extra mile, and I'll meet you at the finish line.

When we imagine rooms being glamorous and polished, we tend to see them more like black-and-white movies, but that's such a bore.

Want to be original? Chart a course for glamour that's based on the contemporary world, not some 1930s rerun. Add sheen and luster with semi- or high-gloss paint to bring an effervescent energy.

A spirited mixture of furniture and materials loosens up a room.

Throw out the standardized assembly of cast members and explore your options. The last thing a big upholstered sofa wants is to be paired with two big upholstered chairs. Ready to dissect this sofa? The tiger velvet is way expensive, and everyone wants it somewhere. What to do? The cognac-colored leather is pretty snappy too, and rumor has it that every man lusts for a leather something. The solution? Combine the two. I'm not sure I'm strong enough for an entire sofa made of leather, and there's an eighties thing with all animal prints, all the time. This combo addresses the need for both in a super modern way. Leather is the body for structure, tiger velvet is the "cush for your tush" and puts the softest fabrics just where you want them: on the seat and next to your arms and hands. Feel me! Touch me! Heal me!

HAPPY

Happiness is sometimes knowing what to leave out.

When deciding what table to pair with this kitchen island, we tossed out countless options. As I showed the client the four thousandth choice, it dawned on me that actually a table wasn't needed after all. Instead of playing by the rule book, we went with our instincts and created the perfect place to perch and enjoy a cup of coffee.

This library is the happy-face emoji of rooms.

Well, at least it is for me! Every material here fills me with glee—the nailhead trim on printed cotton walls, the luminous lacquered persimmon ceiling, the strapwork on the sofa, the painted floor. It's going the extra mile on details like these that transform a space into a place worth relishing and make the additional thought, work, and expense absolutely worth it.

This unforgettable wall could have simply been a console and a pair of lamps.

If that had been the case, the room would have been just another pretty living room. Instead this wall of art creates a genuine enthusiasm that bubbles up every time you enter. Of course, this is commanding twentieth-century blue-chip art, but the same effect is easily created with a set of collages all framed and matted similarly, then hung tightly to fill the wall. Much easier to pull off than the more expected salon hang, this type of execution takes real guts. But once you embrace the idea, it will leave you hankering for more walls to cover.

HAPPY

HAPPY

Pattern takes just as much confidence as color.

While you can go with something timid or muted, it's much more satisfying to be bold. Pattern on white linen is the easiest way to make a big statement with very little risk. It's never pretentious or preposterous even when it's packing a punch, which is why it can bring so much joy to room.

Chairs in frame can cause such fright.

Generally, people believe only heavily stuffed upholstered chairs are comfortable. I prove them wrong with the classical klismos chair, truly one of the hallmarks of so many of my rooms. The yoked back allows flexibility in how you can occupy it while completely enveloping you. Take note of the pair of ottomans on casters waiting on the sidelines to be put to use as well. All soldiers at the ready!

There's a good reason gingham is one of my signatures.

This proven material works high or low, bringing exuberance, spirit, and style to any home. From a child's delightful playroom to Valentino's vision of soigné living in Rome, this universally happy pattern comes in so many variations you can easily find one that suits any room. While we're on the subject, you've probably noticed there's more than one pattern at play here. The large-scale "Bird and Basket" pattern on the ottoman works nicely with the gingham because it's the opposite of the intimate black-and-white check. Patterns mix well together when they are of significantly different scales.

HAPPY

What makes me most happy about this child's room is the jubilant Albert Hadley–designed wallpaper, aptly named Happy.

But beyond that personal favorite, I could write an entire ode to the joys of a niche bed. The built-in structure gives a sense of security at bedtime, while the theatrical curtain is meant for creativity at playtime. It's a bunk bed taken to a whole new level.

Art can animate a room even if it isn't trophy art.

These prints, hung in multiples, electrify what would otherwise be a somber dining room. The jolt of color that artwork can add doesn't have to come at a high price or be an original, one-of-a-kind masterpiece. Just pick what brings a smile to your face and don't worry about whether it matches.

HAPPY

Libraries can be many things, but rarely does happy spring to mind.

But by eschewing the traditional red walls and dark woods, you can quickly move from serious to joyous. A turmeric-colored rug adds warmth and excitement, while a series of reclaimed, bleached French doors reference the type of paneling expected in a book-lined room. The palette of cinnabar, taupe, and café au lait comes from the book spines. All the signals of a library are here, but it's a completely contemporary reimagination of one. Delightful twists on design classics like this are waiting to be discovered in every room in the house, so don't be afraid to rewrite the ending!

HAPPY

Terrified of adding pattern?

Try something in blue and white. Whole books have been written about the power of this color duo. Whole careers have been based on its allure. This particular chrysanthemum pattern even has its own presidential history—the original version was made for Jacqueline Kennedy when she refreshed the White House with legendary decorator Sister Parish. If that isn't a seal of style approval, I don't know what is.

Sophisticated rooms are often admired—but not much more than that.

While conjuring a highly refined room that's still inviting, it's important to remember to keep some elements loose and breezy. The peachy pink ceiling is light and not too stuffy, as are the relaxed linen covers with a swishy skirt on the sofa and chair. Speaking of furniture, notice how the crescent sofa isn't slammed up against a wall? That helps keep things convivial, along with the scaled-down eighteenth-century Scottish mantel, which is more of a tactile invitation. It could have easily been paired with a gilded, look-at-me mirror, but no need when there's the option of a clean, contemporary portal instead. Definitely worth more than a second look!

HAPPY

HAPPY

In a room of straight lines, a wavy headboard delivers just enough graphic juxtaposition to enliven the mood.

This detail doesn't need to call attention to itself with a bold color choice or contrasting trim; it simply exists in its own delightful way. Another dreamy addition to the bed are the upholstered lumbar pillows, which allow you to sit up in bed and read. Just toss them aside when you're ready to turn out the lights.

Formal dining rooms are all about entertaining, but most of the time they're not being used.

I animated this one by including an absolutely jubilant large-scale pattern on the chairs. Indulging in its forty-eight-inch repeat, the fronts, backs, and seats all come from different motifs, adding to the overall playfulness. Going a step further, a curved banquette rounds out the seating options. Even when dinner isn't being served, there's always something going on here.

An unbridled, unaffected combination of color always sparks delight.

Two of my favorite colors, vermilion and Persian blue, are strong enough to carry a whole room while allowing the rest of the pieces to remain neutral and monochromatic. No matter what your favorite colors are, incorporating them into a scheme is guaranteed to brighten your mood and add confidence.

HAPPY

Elsie de Wolfe, Syrie Maugham, and Bunny Mellon had something in common besides their exquisite taste: they all believed in painting their furniture. Nothing enlivens a brown chest of drawers quite like a coat or two of white paint, and there's a design pedigree to prove it. To tell you the truth, any wood can be painted after a light sanding. Let's not forget, this is paint, not lacquer, which is a much different, more complex process. So seeing a few telltale brushstrokes in the finished pieces does have its upside. Paint away.

COLORFUL

Color represents confidence. Wimpy people don't paint their walls persimmon or hang yards of cinnabar curtains. But it doesn't take as much guts as you might think, especially once I let you in on a few secrets. First of all, there's no such thing as colors that don't go together. Move that aside. There's no color I couldn't or wouldn't work with. Try me! And I'm simply ecstatic when I discover a new color. My palette is always evolving, and the colors I like today have nothing to do with the colors I liked yesterday.

There are numerous steps toward accepting color. You need to find your comfort level or zone. There's a myth that if you embrace color it has to be everywhere in your house, but color can be used sporadically and intimately. Maybe it's only a countertop in a bold shade of red or the back of a bookshelf in coral—trust me, these moments make all the difference.

Also, mixing color isn't so tricky when you look at them tonally. Notice, I said mixing—not matching. To create harmony, I try to look at color in terms of saturation instead of relying on typical color families. If I took a black-and-white photo of a room I had filled with color, you couldn't tell the difference because the "colors" are the same tonal shade. It opens up so many possibilities and is far more interesting than pulling colors out of a single pattern to connect a room.

When most people think of color, they grab paint. Picking the wall color is the very last thing I do. But really you can apply color anywhere—It could be a bright rug on the floor, a ravishing shade at the window, or even the most enchanting lacquered ceiling. Go about your next decorating project with this in mind, and you'll blush at the staggering results.

Ever been in a house that feels like the "It's a Small World" ride at Disneyland?

Every room introduces a new, completely disconnected theme; color must flow from room to room. An intense blue entrance connects to a white living room through the consistency of a painted floor. Plus, the pattern on the settee has a touch of the gourd color found in the curtains and then again on the sofa in the next room.

The first lesson about coloring that you learn as a child is to stay inside the lines.

Big news—the same holds true for decorating. By containing this super saturated red inside the cupboard, it plays nicely with pixilation of turquoise on the walls in the quatrefoil-patterned wallpaper. So think about small or hidden places where you can go wild with color—what about the inside of a drawer in chromium yellow or the back of bookcase in teal blue?

COLORFUL

There's no question that black is a color.

These painted floors anchor the room and provide a foil for pattern, which would be only half as strong without it. As an added bonus, light bounces off the dark floor and makes the hall even brighter.

A room painted this boldly takes confidence, but don't burden it with too much color.

Keep the trim, furniture, and flowers more muted and tempered so every element doesn't shout.

If you're thinking of experimenting with color, start with the library.

Book spines already have more colors than any other room in the house. From there, try another safe bet with yellow curtains. It's natural to look toward a window and wish for the color of the golden sun. And let's talk a bit about breaking up color: if you're too timid to use a solid block of color for upholstery but don't want to default to pattern, use a tape trim to add geometric structure to upholstery. It creates a series of small "blocks" instead of one big block.

COLORFUL

Flowers will
always be the
easiest way
to inject
color and life
into a room.
Don't worry about getting
too matchy-matchy with your
decor and arrangements.
Instead, follow nature's
seasonal cues—go with
magnolia branches in winter
and yellow daffodils or lilacs
in spring. There's no wrong in
colorful, seasonal changes.

Never match the color of your artwork to the design of your room.

Paintings are not wallpaper or backdrop or background. This holds true for good art and bad art—and I've worked with both. As long as you love the art, it can go anywhere in the house where it brings a flash of unexpected color.

COLORFUL

COLORFUL

There's no
reason a closet
can't have
a little splash
of color.
Of course, painting all the walls
will alter the way your clothes
and you appear—but an
accessory here and there, like
this blue glass mirror frame,
certainly has its merits. Choose
a few pieces of furniture and
some objects to liven up the
space where so many important
decisions are made.

Start with the fabric not the paint deck, especially if you're confident with color.

I select all my fabrics before addressing the walls. Here, the bold cloud-blue sofa needed an equally amped up daffodil yellow to tango. If I hear one more decorator mention butter yellow, I'm going to change my profession to dentist.

COLORFUL

Orange and magenta upholstery anchor this vast room, while sage green curtains open it up to the garden view.

The orange fabric at the French doors grabs for attention as it directs traffic to the terrace beyond. Consider all of these as "directional signals" that help the user better understand what to do in a room.

The link between the chartreuse-green walls and the sky-blue sofa is in the fabric on two pillows where both colors exist.

Start with the colors you love, then find one fabric to connect the dots. It's that simple.

How do you unite colors without relying on pattern?

Most people split hairs over comple-
menting or coordinating colors, but
what's best is to bundle your saturated
hues and your pastels together.
Here, I went for strong, jewel tones
for the fabrics with a neutral China
matting on the floor to break up
the intensity. If I had mixed in, say, a
petal pink, it simply wouldn't harm-
onize like the cranberry tablecloth
and the cantaloupe chair do.

A colorful entry establishes a sense of arrival, while not fatiguing the residents with a bold shade in a room that sees everyday, long-term use.

This cobalt blue paint was dry-brushed to create texture and is accented by a mahogany handrail, which reflects the exposed wood elements in the painted and stenciled floors. The curtains are two different colors of the same washed linen. Many entrance halls are drafty places because doors are opened and closed throughout fall and winter months. Hanging curtains at doorways (correctly called "portieres") reduces the draft that swooshes in from one room to another. This design is based on historical precedent. It also gives you another place for a fantastic pair of curtains! Works for me.

COLORFUL

COLORFUL

Don't miss the chance for an unexpected dose of color.

I never do—even when it comes to blackout shades. There are so many more options than the standard black, white, or gray. Here, barn red complements the vernacular of the house while both adding a surprising hue at the window and punctuating the Indian cotton cloth curtains.

COLORFUL

There's a lot of hand-wringing over countertops, and most people just default to a boring, antiseptic white.

Why not embrace the opportunity to interject color and personality into the kitchen? Like a welcoming red-leather banquette at the 21 Club, this jazzy laminate surface banded in stainless steel adds pizazz. Confident colors such as indigo blue, chromium yellow, and emerald green do the trick just as well and should have you rethinking that trip to the marble-slab yard.

A lot of people overcommit to color.

And then all of a sudden everything is jumbled into one big, exhausting mess. You need to insert selective, strategic punctuations of white to balance color saturation. The white matting around the artwork, the white border on the fireplace, and the white sculpture on the wall are all there to do a very important job.

COLORFUL

Introducing color doesn't mean you have to invest in all the colors.

Just one bold hue can make a major difference, especially red, which can make everything snap to attention. This crimson lacquered table creates a powerful counterpoint to the barn wood that surrounds it. The reaction is picked up in the snappy hue of the cube tables and the tomatoes, thereby becoming visual markers that connect various elements of the large space. Added bonus: the gloss against the matte of the untreated lath walls and timber posts accentuates the contrast.

COLORFUL

This room would have half the energy with a sisal rug on the floor.

The bright bolt of color from the dhurrie carries the neutral-colored tiger velvet and leather upholstery, as well as the white walls. With today's modernist architecture defined by very little millwork, there are few guidelines to create a frame for color. Oftentimes the rug is the only way to inject color and break up the white box.

Add a splash of color to austere white rooms
by covering your chairs in an unexpected Indian
textile with strong shades of red and green.
Consider it a start and a finish all in one.

PERSONAL

This is a biggie. I can say this over and over again and not say it enough: we have to understand that the goal of decorating is to personalize your house. Don't build a showhouse or a model apartment inspired by someone else's fantasy of how you should live. Instead, be true to yourself and create a home that you want to live in.

When I begin with a new client, I ask them to go into my design library and find things they're innately drawn to—not based on any room, scheme, or plan. Just go with your gut, and show me what you love. You can easily do this by leafing through design books. Nothing gives me more joy than seeing a design book filled with Post-it notes and tabs of favorite ideas. Instagram, Pinterest, magazines—these are all wonderful resources for collecting ideas. Then, figure out what they all have in common. Is it blue rooms, shiny things, antiques? Now, you're gaining insight into your personal style.

Personal collections are also key to giving a home personality. No matter how modest, they are incredibly valuable when putting your stamp on a room. I'll go into deep storage with a client, practically excavating their lives, because you never know what you'll find. It may be a quirky old portrait of a relative, trophies and ribbons from competitions long past, flowers pressed over the years—all of these items have merit in telling the story of a fascinating life. When curated and displayed in a thoughtful manner, the possibilities are endless, from my signature wonder table to tiny shelves above a fireplace.

Don't forget—you start and finish with personality. For me, it's the first step in deciding what direction a project will take, as well as the last layer when finishing a room with elements of soul and spirit. What's critically important is that this part of decorating requires you to have a bit of fun. You must find joy in this part of the process because it will resonate in the final result. And that's exactly how you go about putting your stamp on it!

I've never heard a four-year-old ask to meet with a decorator, but that doesn't mean children's rooms shouldn't be flooded with personality.

They need stimulating places to grow up in and a world to call their own.

Show your personality as soon as guests walk in the door.

A display of colorful umbrellas exhibits creativity and personal style. It doesn't have to be umbrellas—any signature touch will not go overlooked or be forgotten. Another vastly underrated opportunity is family photos. I love seeing them amassed in an entry, which, as its name suggests, should be a starting point for getting to know you.

PERSONAL

PERSONAL

When you have a compelling view, do everything in your power to showcase it.

This verdant green setting can be more fully appreciated with furniture scaled low to the ground, such as the canoe chairs and the table designed to a correspondingly suitable height, as well as screens with the cross bracer built at the top rather than the bottom, so nothing gets in the way of absorbing the surroundings. All of this from a room that was once just a porte cochere.

Typically paneled over, the gap between the chimney breast and the flue provides an incredible opportunity for an intimate vignette of personal objects.

It's a valuable space that can easily be reclaimed to display collections, from seashells to porcelain, although, for obvious reasons, I don't recommend books. It's perfectly situated for a closer look when stoking or simply admiring the fire.

PERSONAL

Thoughtful details can make just about any space feel intimate.

Spontaneous decoration with postcards and mementos tucked into a bathroom mirror becomes a mini art display ready to be discovered or swapped out for a new installation at any moment. Shells that look like souvenirs from a beach vacation are actually pill boxes for stashes of ibuprofen, while an opaline glass jar scooped up at a tag sale houses cotton balls.

Take the very best of the past and optimistically look forward.

The walls of this enchanting bedroom are covered in atmospheric de Gournay hand-painted paper.
It was a ravishing starting point but not the finish. By adding rivulets of molten gold, deftly rendered
by acclaimed artist Nancy Lorenz, the transformation is far more personal and modern.

This grand dining room in a historic New York apartment building screams late nineteenth century.

So how do we muffle those shouts? With personality, of course. By displaying the owner's twentieth-century photography collection, we're jolted into the modern day, even if I couldn't resist using some William Morris wallpaper. But that's the whole point of this room. It's as if generations of a family had lived here and each added their own perspective to the place.

PERSONAL

Don't make the mistake of only using your dining table for formal dinners.

Use the surface to set out a buffet for an outdoor meal. Find a way to incorporate this piece into everyday life, and be sure to always dress it with decorative elements like vases, flowers, or bowls of fruit. Remember that there's no rule that every chair around the table has to match, if you even have chairs at all!

PERSONAL

PERSONAL

Collections are only as good as how much they're appreciated.

Guitars installed as art are also accessible instruments to be enjoyed. Collect what you love, and remember, put them on display so guests can better understand your personality.

It doesn't get more clear-headed than this all-white bedroom.

A symphony of beautiful silhouettes, this room is absolutely content in how orderly and settled in it is.
That kind of comfort yields happiness, because everything feels in and of itself. But I must admit, when
the clients said they wanted an all-white room, the first thing I did was paint the ceiling a pale blue.

Boom!

Adding layers of personal
objects, books, accessories,
flowers, and even a few
statement lampshades makes
all the difference between
a good and great room.

PERSONAL

People tend to think of personality as highly effervescent and loud, but it can also be nuanced and small and quiet.

These vases in celadon greens and blues, which are only a few inches high, reveal personality in whispers, not shouts. That invitation to lean in carries throughout the room with a diminutive panel-glass folding screen that doesn't block sight lines and low-hung paintings meant to be enjoyed while seated.

Why do people obsess over floral centerpieces when a trip to the market can net much more original results?

Flowers will be long gone in a few days, while fruit looks fresh for longer. And don't stop there—what about that seashell collection from beach vacations or the small set of tureens your mother started assembling in the 1960s? A personal connection to a room can begin with thoughtful designs for tabletops (dining or other) and evolve to other areas that very naturally extend the statement.

PERSONAL

Here's a bit of advice—adding more personality to your house begins with a good thorough edit.

Take the five hundred items you have in your life and figure out what the most important ones are, the ones that truly tell a story. By eliminating the clutter, the remaining pieces gain more significance. For this client, we highlighted the best of their belongings—a nineteenth-century chair, a handsome pair of bronze cocktail tables, an English Regency bench with a tiger print—which had once been lost in an overwhelming mix. Now, you can truly see more of them by having less of them.

Did someone really tell you that lusterware doesn't go with majolica?

Well, they were wrong. Putting components together for a tabletop is a lot easier than doing the same for a room. Simple rule: match your personality or mood with the objects you select and craft a great story.

Small touches make a big impact when setting the table.

Something as simple and straightforward as kitchen twine with a sage leaf enhances your tabletop while giving a nod to the pork chops that are about to be served. Don't have linen? Try this personal touch with paper napkins and you'll be even more satisfied with the results!

When you start with the gold standard of an architectural backdrop, don't let decorating get in the way.

This contemporary white backdrop with flashes of black cabinetry needs to own the moment, but there's still room for some degree of personality that doesn't camouflage the conceit. An expert curation of the owner's pottery tells that story. What's key here is not the value of the pieces selected, but how they work together as a group, changing and modulating in scale. Together, the collection gives that whiff of a human touch and leads the eye to the massive tribal sculpture in the courtyard beyond.

PERSONAL

Building a narrative around a personal collection is more than just buying random pieces that strike your fancy.

To be a collector, you must be focused and buy in multiples, all with the advantage of learning more about a particular type of object while amassing it. These clients sought out horn cups on travels around the world. The result: a collection of four dozen or so pieces perfectly suited to their home, which happens to also be filled with a beautiful melody of tonal grays.

A room with a personal collection displayed will always feel lived in.

These clients had assembled a menagerie of hand-carved birds. Previously they had been sprinkled in rooms throughout the house, and I have to admit the effect was a bit Hitchcockian. When displayed clustered together, perched on the shelf and offset against a selection of white glazed ceramics, they're simply fan-friggin'-tastic. This handsome room became that much better with these little touchstones of something the owners loved and collected.

When I completed this dining room, it was a strong, wonderful success. I went back a few days later and a pair of monumental bronze floor lamps had appeared. What was powerfully important was that the client had found them and they spoke to her. They were perfect because she put them there, and they injected her personal touch and love of the unexpected. These types of serendipitous finds add enormous personality, and everyone loves an element of surprise.

Truth be told, when preparing for a lunch or dinner with friends, I like to lay out all the plates and silver a few days—or even a week—beforehand. It's fun to mix patterns and periods that accentuate the table settings and reflect the menu, the mood, and the occasion.

What could be more welcoming than a roaring fire?

Fireplaces bring not only warmth, they ignite all the senses. Light-years more distinct than the expected console table, this fireplace once faced into the room on the opposite side of the wall. By closing it up in the living room, we opened up a beautiful opportunity to bring warmth and personality to the entry, creating a real sense of arrival that is enhanced by the use of Delft tiles for the fireplace slip, a more unique and economical material than marble.

White is just right in an entry hall of brown timber.

To better appreciate the original wooden architecture,

I furnished the space with various shades of a crisp, clean palette.

We all know the drill in a library.

The room often lacks so much originality that they're practically interchangeable from house to house. These clients were determined to have a library but not a traditional one. To create a more modern room that everyone could enjoy, we designed an enormous sofa far larger than standard issue. I then reimagined the bookcases as freestanding rather than built-in to loosen things up. A few elements will always remain essential (note the small sconces that illuminate both books and reader), but we're only as modern as our past, which is ripe for reinvention.

LIGHTER & BRIGHTER

Of all the decorating trends that come and go, one has been growing exponentially over the last twenty years with no signs of receding—it's making every room lighter and brighter. Quite frankly, I consider it the tsunami of modern decorating, and the wave is only getting higher and more powerful.

This sweeping change is driven by the technological and engineering advancements made in the way we build our houses. Through insulation and heating and cooling systems, homes can afford to have larger windows despite the climate conditions. As a result, we're not only letting more light in, but the way we decorate these spaces has changed as well. Heavy curtains that used to insulate rooms are now simply added as a matter of taste. Floors piled with rugs don't keep the chill out as much as they make a decorative statement. But with all this freedom, we still are seeking out ways to brighten spaces even more.

The first thing that pops into anyone's head is a bucket of white paint. Given my love of full-throttle color, you might be inclined to think I would dismiss this notion in an instant. But you'd be wrong. I'm the biggest advocate of purposeful whites—white not by default, but with good reason. Ever painted a floor a glossy white? Absolute heaven, bouncing light this way and that. Even old brown furniture perks up with a coat of paint, giving the whole room an instant face lift. And white makes for the most illuminating backdrop for a room flooded with color.

Details and small objects can play a huge role in adding sparkle as well. Burnished gilded frames, crystal, cut glass, and mirrors reflect light throughout a space like no one's business. They truly animate and brighten a space, especially when paired with metal hardware, hinges, and knobs. So, don't be so quick to call up the architect to add that wall of sheet glass, especially with all the bright ideas I'm about to share.

No one is going to question whether this room was intentionally painted all white.

The strong graphic quality of the inky black band holding the firewood shows purpose and makes the white even brighter. But if you're going to immerse yourself in an all-white envelope, please pick a warm shade of white with some body (Benjamin Moore White Dove is a favorite!). Otherwise you'll take on the sickly pallor you acquire when perusing the frozen-food section in a grocery store.

You know how the flight attendant always says the nearest exit may be behind you?

Well, the same goes for daylight—sometimes it's behind you. This banquet in a bay window allows for dining with the light at your back. That way, it can add shimmer to the crystal and silver on the table or brighten up the morning paper.

LIGHTER & BRIGHTER

Whether it's auction purchases or tag-sale finds, cut glass, pressed glass, etched glass, and even the unfortunately named depression glass makes a room sparkle. Displayed as a whole collection or scattered here and there, their incandescent quality makes accessorizing with these beautiful objects compelling day or night. I love them in groups, empty or full.

When paneling this room became too costly, the alternative proved just as dazzling (perhaps even more so!)—without the expense.

We conceived that outlines of nailheads on the wall could suggest the form of traditional paneling. This addition animates the fabric walls and draws the eye around the room. It's fairly simple to achieve—you just make a cardboard template to establish the pattern before hammering away. And, why yes, those are the same nailheads repeated at the base of the chair.

If you're going for contrast, why not take it to the extreme?

A dense, dark backdrop enhances the white and ivory furniture to make this whole room brighter. All the lightness comes to the foreground, and the rest disappears. You can use any dark saturated color—indigo, eggplant, tobacco—as long as you hold true and coat all the walls. I used to keep the moldings white, but now we've taken to painting them dark as well. Also, the finish must have at least an eggshell sheen or brighter luster. Yes, it can be terrifying, but once all the furniture is in place the success will be as plain as black and white.

LIGHTER & BRIGHTER

The joy of an all-white room can be absolute heaven.

But be warned—it can easily backfire and come off as empty, vacuous, and anonymous. What fills the void here is personality! You have to enliven the room with furniture and objects that shine. So, go ahead and paint the walls and floors white, but know that the burden falls on you to populate the space with striking pieces.

It may seem completely counter-intuitive, but these dark tobacco walls and sofa actually make this solarium even brighter. The contrast emphasizes the light that streams through the floor-to-ceiling windows, so you can fully appreciate the fantastic curtain wall and light-filled urban oasis. If everything were white, the effect wouldn't be as dramatic or effective.

LIGHTER & BRIGHTER

You're not obligated to lacquer an entire room.

With a surface ignited with abalone shell, ormolu, gilding, or lacquer, a small piece of furniture is a fantastic way to add enough shimmer to make an impact. Just one strategic purchase, such as this Ming ebony lacquer side table with mother-of-pearl details, does the trick. Or go for something with a mirrored top or glossy metal hardware and banding—you'll be astonished by just how much shine something so small can add.

Please join me in my crusade to take the guilt out of gilding.

Gold furniture and flourishes get such a bad rap as being nouveau riche, when truly it's quite the opposite when used with nuance and restraint. Incredibly sophisticated, the gleam of gold, whether on a chair or picture frame, gives a room a ravishing glow.

Ever had one of those mornings when you want to just roll out of bed and have a soak?

Well, that's exactly what this bedside tub is meant for here. Yes, I admit it's a daring move. But it comes from the time when the English converted old manors to include baths, and they just added them in the bedroom. It's really studio living on the most sophisticated level, especially when you take into account the seaside accents of blue and white porcelain, Madagascar cloth, and shimmering green curtains.

LIGHTER & BRIGHTER

The modern concept of opening up a living room into a dining room is a surefire way to add air and light to an interior.

This often leads to one big, bland, jumbled multipurpose room, but here, the spaces are kept distinct yet connected. Portieres define the division and allow you to close the curtains when the functions need to be kept separate. On the ceiling, a soffit also demarks where one space ends and the other begins, while the use of similar textures, materials, and values keep the two rooms cohesive.

Full disclosure: I've used this decorator's trick many times before.

A mirror floating in front of a window allows for natural light to fill a room while providing a bit of privacy. Unlike a picture or painting, a mirror actually works well when hung this way. Plus, it's fantastically easy to implement with just two little hooks and chains. Best of all, everyone's reflection looks best when they are illuminated by daylight.

Just how many pairs of French doors does a person really need?

There's been an enormous push to add lots of French doors to houses because of their obvious light-adding benefit. Don't be fooled. Develop your furniture plan as if the doors are actually windows and don't worry if the sofa cuts in front of them. Let real comfort and good conversation drive your decision making.

LIGHTER & BRIGHTER

LIGHTER & BRIGHTER

We all need a
mirror over
a sink, but
doesn't just
hanging it up
there get dull?

For this beachside home, I
decided to use a bit of wit and
rig up some sailing rope to
hang these mirrors above the
double vanity. Suddenly, there's
a little humanity in the room.

Not all dining rooms need to be indoors.

Pay just as much attention to decorating an outdoor room, and you'll enjoy more meals alfresco. Real furniture that could easily live inside plays a huge part in setting the stage. So do a framed mirror, thoughtful lighting fixtures, and an all-weather rug that mimics antique carpets.

It's true there is such a thing as too much light.

This Nantucket entry hall has the most glorious view from the bay window, but it problematically overwhelmed the space: like a slingshot, you were catapulted through the entrance hall, past the garden, and straight to the ocean. It was just too much of a good thing. There was no sense of arrival—as soon as you entered the house you were already gone. The solution was to nestle a banquet in that space, the equivalent of a window seat. The vista is still there to be admired, but only once you've allowed the house to embrace you first.

There's a good reason café curtains are such an iconic part of my work.

They truly give you the best of both worlds—allowing light to flood a room while still offering a bit of privacy. They're most effective when made from unlined cotton, cotton voile, or linen. This style also lowers the sight line, exaggerating the scale of a room and giving the illusion of a much higher ceiling.

You can be fearless about using dark colors as a backdrop if you understand the contrast of lightness against it.

A murky, mossy, dense garden wallpaper only comes to life with the addition of a bit of brightness to illuminate it. I find this technique especially commendable in a bedroom, where you want the edges to fall away when the lights are off. Need further proof? Take a gander at that portrait of a little girl in a white dress absolutely shining in an inky setting.

LIGHTER & BRIGHTER

LIGHTER & BRIGHTER

To bounce light down a hallway with few windows, paint the floor a super glossy white. Now, any light coming through an open door will ricochet throughout the space. Special porch and decking enamel is engineered for the wear-and-tear of this surface. No longer is a passageway doomed to be nothing more than a dark and bleak warren of doors.

Once a terrace, this solarium gets its appeal from more than just the soaring windows.

All kinds of tricks are in play to draw you into the space. The French doors provide a warm welcome, while the camelback of the sofa and the ivory throw punctuate the focus. The hand-blocked cotton voile curtains allow the light to still pour in while giving just enough privacy. And the ultimate touch is the gilded sun mirror, a reference that clearly needs no explanation.

Just like these Robert Longo black-and-white drawings that grab your attention, this snappy, snazzy dining room has a crispness that can't be dismissed.

The graphic palette adds structure and a sense of architecture to the sleek space. Nothing here is superfluous, but every detail is strategically calibrated to support that graphic punch, from the herringbone floor to the subtle tonal stripe on the wall.

LIGHTER & BRIGHTER

LIGHTER & BRIGHTER

A steel casement shower opens up a bathroom and brings the illusion of sunlight into the entire room.

An all-marble or tile enclosure would make the room feel smaller and leave you in the dark. By placing towel bars at the far end of the enclosure, there's no need to dash across the room in order to dry off. Plus, surprise surprise, the towels really don't get wet.

An oversize lamp certainly makes a room lighter and brighter.

In this kitchen, acclaimed lighting designer John Wigmore devised a dramatically scaled-up table lampshade
for a kitchen island. Two conical shades float above the island, penetrating the space with light while
giving a sense of intimacy. Create this scene stealer by simply replacing your run-of-the-mill downlights.

SEXY

I'm tempted to say that sexy needs no introduction and just leave it at that. But the more I've swirled it around in my head, the more I realize how much it actually does, more than any other attribute elucidated in the chapters of this book.

Sexy is a very big word to throw around, and I'm not talking about rose petals, candlelit bedrooms, and come-hither looks. Sexy takes effort and intelligence. It's not spontaneous, and it takes some planning and energy. In designing a home, shape, texture, and color are all paths on the road to sexy. As much as a curvaceous line is sexy, so is the right angle. I especially like to pair the two by placing an urn on top of a sharp-edged pedestal. Linens, velvets, cashmeres—there's a world of materials that breathe sexy into a space. So many colors are inherently sexy. Reds, especially orange-based shades, hit all the marks, but blue-based reds are a bit too icy.

And let's not forget how compelling small gestures can be. There's plenty of opportunity to deliver a sexy message that is close to us. I like to think of a table set with an abundance of candles and lots of gleaming surfaces to bounce the flickering light. Also, something unexpected goes a long way. Just think of how that out-of-nowhere flirty wink can stop you in your tracks. In the home, that can come in the form of a hidden detail noticed only by those who look closely enough—maybe it's the color on the inside of a drawer or a well-stocked bar tucked into a nook in a hallway. The opportunities are endless. Let the seduction begin.

You have to agree, all of these components look hot together.

It's the perfect proof that intelligence is sexy—even in a coat hall. The robin's-egg blue wallpaper came first. Since it's such a narrow hall with such an eclectic mix, the bright red tape with nailheads connects the space and holds all the elements together. Now, the pieces can mix and mingle—the ikats and trims are chatting, all the red swatches are talking it up, all while the masks and art are connecting with the leopard carpet. Every piece chosen for a room should be able to strike up a conversation with something else. If not, rethink your choice, because you've now invited that party guest alone into the room.

I'll admit it, day-to-night sexy is a challenge even for an old pro.

This library is able to make the transition for many reasons. First, the walls aren't black lacquer; instead, they're the darkest shade of brown. Let's call it black coffee, and it's sublimely countered by the whites of the mantel, the Fortuny sofa, and the trim paint, along with that shock of green on the chair. The dark walls just recede like the edges of a stage set, especially at night when the room becomes a glamorous, urbane pad. But the best part is there's no hangover in the morning. It's just back to being its energized, sexy self.

SEXY

Sexy rooms are more about what you take off than put on.

The architectural arches and French doors were so beautiful they needed no further embellishment. Good architecture compliments great decoration.

Don't fall victim to hanging a typical chandelier over the table before you explore the options.

An unexpected sculpture like this mobile is much more flirtatious than the standard route. Light the space with a few pin lights instead, and watch the sculpture get the party started.

SEXY

Full disclosure: This is why you hire a decorator.

It took the clients six months to agree to this mirrored dining room, and it's by far the best decision we made on the project. These molten, reflective walls are dazzling with their mysterious broken reflections and ripples. Not to be confused with those dreadful 1970s and '80s sheet-mirrored rooms, this dining room harkens back to the belle epoque. During the day, the shimmering surfaces bounce natural light around the room and give a glimpse of the view from every angle in the room. In the evening, flickering candlelight is magnified and dinner guests bask in a rosy glow. And for when all this allure and seduction gets to be too much, there's a blush-pink linen curtain that enwraps the room, transforming the space into a tented pavilion. How's that for dinner and a show?

There's something about the color Roman Red that just gets my blood going.

Dipping a room in a single voluptuous shade of red, and color-matching the curtains, brings out the interior's best assets. With the backdrops the same shade as the window treatments, your eye is drawn to the details. Think of this as your little black dress, but in red!

There's something to be admired about a curvaceous urn on a pedestal.

The contrast of this rectangular base accentuates the urn's graceful form. To call even more attention to those lithesome lines, a tobacco-colored quilted moving blanket forms an alluring backdrop for the creamy, lacquered-linen plaster finish of the vessel. The overall effect creates a focal point at the end of a hallway that beckons you closer, and if sexy doesn't bring you closer then what's the point?

It's not a cliché to say that red is a sexy color.

It's a fact. Think roses, hearts, velvet—the list goes on. Another fact: the color works better in a bedroom than any other room in the house. Just don't get carried away. Too much red can backfire, so stick with the walls and maybe the curtains. After that, feel free to throw any color you can think of at it. Don't worry—red can handle it. Avoid blue-based reds (you'll look dead in bed) and select within a spectrum of orange-based reds (smokin' in the sack!).

SEXY

SEXY

There's nuance
and superb
subtlety to this
dressing room.
Of course, by taking that path,
the risk is that some of the
information can get lost. The
details really need to punctuate the
space, since they drive it's success.
Without the nail trim on the
tabletop and gunmetal rail above
the doors, the finesse of the fabric-
covered walls would simply vanish.
The eye needs to land somewhere
in a room, and it's your duty to
map out the points of interest
with laser-sharp focus.

Understatement is the key to doing sexy right.

This dining room seduces the eye with a litany of small, thoughtful gestures such as the diminutive Murano chandelier. We generally start the furniture plan with a polished wood table, but I like to include a mix of unexpected, bold materials on the backs of the chairs.

SEXY

There's a lot to be said about a furnished bathroom.

Notice the discreet elevated tub in black soapstone at the back of the room. Other than that, there's no indication that this isn't just another lovely sitting room. If you can, save room for a chair, settee, or chaise to domesticate these rooms. I'm stark-raving crazy about carpeted bathrooms. They are comfortable and practical. Bath mats (the oven mitts of carpeting) can slip and slide; wall-to-wall does not.

SEXY

Often overlooked in favor of color or pattern, shape plays just as important a role in establishing the mood of a room. Here, a seductive effect is created by repeating the curvaceous line of the staircase in the arm of the iron settee, the inlaid border of the floor, and the profile of the pottery. Instead of grouping items by color, pattern, or period, try assembling them by shape and form. There is a common language they share that can act as a kind of connective tissue to all the elements.

Voluptuous curves may have cornered the market on sexy, but orderly angles have their place there, too.

Symmetry and repeated patterns provide balance and order. Something tells me
sexy is not spontaneous, but rather it is thoughtful and considered.

Sexy has gender.

Olive-colored velvet-clad walls, burnished-bronze upholstery, and the gleam of polished precious metals bring a clear masculine sensibility to this bedroom. Remember that colors send a message about the occupant.

The expected is never sexy.

This urn was white when we purchased it, but it needed a new look to make it less run of the mill. I decided I'd rather paint it than put flowers in it. In light blue, it took on a whole new, sexier persona. So please don't look at something and expect it to exist the way you see it. Open your eyes, and realize when there's a makeover moment just waiting to happen. We all live for some kind of transformation or before-and-after story.

Romance resides in every detail of this bedroom.

From the light green accent on the leading edge of the curtains to the abundance of nailheads on the headboard, everything here is designed to draw you in for a closer look. Sexy makes you look twice.

SEXY

SEXY

Not every cabinet needs to conceal a television.

A tucked-away bar brings an old-fashioned glamour to any room. Just be sure to keep it stocked with all the essentials, including napkins, glassware, and garnishes. For goodness' sake, be sure to tell your guests where this bar is and encourage them to help themselves.

I love a visual seducer at the end of a sight line.

Here, a sculptural nest beckons visitors down a corridor into the master bedroom. Who could resist getting a closer look at something so incredibly unique? This is how you should approach every hallway and entryway in your house. It doesn't have to be something quite this daring; it could be as simple as a unique chair at the end of a corridor or a beautiful photo visible through a doorway. Give a strong reason to pull the eye into the next space.

There is a huge difference between warm and cool gray.

Always opt for warm, especially if the backdrop is an intimate setting, to better balance your skin tone. This is a soft and flattering sexy gray that is "bedroom perfect." The crisp white trim and linen bed hangings keep it all fresh.

SEXY

CHARMING

Beauty is something you're born with, and sexy is something you work on, but charm is spontaneous. It reflects who you are. One of the greatest compliments you can give someone is that they are very charming. Likewise, a house filled with charm conjures all good images. Someone once sent me a thank-you note that said, "Your house is the epitome of charm and grace." What a wonderful compliment! I'll treasure the letter always and am even tempted to frame it.

It's more than just packing a house with great pieces. Charming is a level of detail that exists below the surface. It's not self-evident at first, but once you pay attention, all the details, grace, and care put into its design reveal themselves. No one will say "I want my house to be more intimate," but that's exactly what charming rooms are. They have touches that are thoughtful, personal, and autobiographical. As a result, there's a beating heart and a real pulse point. And the home comes alive—spiritually and emotionally—far beyond its physical beauty.

Pattern is probably the easiest tool to harness the potential of charm. When we think of this type of room, there's usually a smattering of florals, stripes, and, naturally, gingham, the most charming fabric of all. Hand-blocked prints bring in a globe-trotting characteristic that nods to a life well traveled. Then there's the layering of collected pieces—mismatched side tables, curious chairs covered in marvelous fabrics, and books and curios galore. All these eclectic layers build a story, and the room begins to hold a conversation of its own.

There's plenty of potential for charming exterior spaces as well. I love a veranda or portiere that's executed with the same level of thoughtful detail as any interior space. With an unexpected chandelier that sways in the breeze or a simple rug that anchors a space, these outdoor rooms come alive and beckon you away from the air-conditioning with their own subtle seductive powers.

As anyone who has ever been to a cocktail party knows, charming people are natural communicators. They're not timid, but they're not blustering. Most of all, they are inherently themselves. And in much the same way, these rooms are just that and don't pretend to be anything but what they truly are.

This hallway could have been an unremarkable pass-through to the more interesting rooms deeper inside.

By including rough straw wall and floor coverings, a smattering of chairs borrowed from the dining room, plus a suite of tole chandeliers, a real sense of character emerges.

We often connote small rooms with heaps of charm.

The only problem is they can start to feel a bit claustrophobic. The trick here is the mirror over the sofa, which reflects the bank of windows on the opposite wall, thereby opening up the interior. Of course, the exposed bare bones of this add-on room with its gray-washed pine only increases the pure and simple joy of the space. Charm is not license to go on a shopping spree in the "cute" aisle of the Sunken Treasure department store. Keep it simple.

Pattern is perhaps the easiest tool to harness the magical power of charm.

Global prints have a beating heart that can't help but add delight. Take for example this Les Indiennes cotton-voile block print: it lends a human element while speaking to a certain global curiosity. When exploring these types of patterns, it's key to add your own touch. The addition of the black trim gives much-needed shape and dimension. Without it, this room just wouldn't have the same crisp structure.

Pattern is a shortcut to charm, but it's not always my weapon of choice.

I'm at my zippiest when pulling colors together because I love them—not simply because they're a small part of some larger multicolored chintz. This room is electrified through the mix of the orange in the rug, a blue chair, and a boysenberry tufted sofa. Don't drive yourself mad trying to find the blue that's in that print. Strike out on your own and watch how strong a room becomes when you pick the colors you love.

CHARMING

CHARMING

I'm indulging myself with this close-up.

I simply cannot get enough of this chair. I love its patina, but it's the expert upholstering that sends me over the moon. Soberly resolved with great finesse, the welt at the plateau is the way this type of seating is meant to be constructed. Plus, the single welting with a contrast biased tape absolutely sings. This isn't just a decorative flourish; a welt actually hides the seam. But do us all a favor and never use double welt. It's lazy, sloppy, and ultimately implies the inability of a qualified workroom to craft this level of detail and finesse. If your upholsterer suggests a double, hop in your car and drive away.

Decorators often speak about creating a moment.

Here, a fabulous tableau unfolds by paying attention not just to what's on the table but what's under it as well. The whole experience is quite curated and scripted, and that's exactly why it holds the viewer's curiosity and asks them to spend just a little longer to discover all the treasures. From the lantern to the bowl to the lampshade with dangling jade beads, they have all been assembled to create a careful narrative. Vary your sizes, from big books to little bowls, so your eye has to constantly search for the next surprise.

How do we make modern architecture less cold and more charming?

It's all about softening angles and diffusing edges. The fireplace ledge would have been all too hard without the addition of Greek mattresses (those soft upholstered pads with their hand-stitching on the outside). The wall of windows is hushed with the curtain folds of elaborate fabrics. Plus, all the antiques with their burnished quality do their part to make this space more livable, while a tea-stained palette with hints of amber makes everything glow with warmth.

CHARMING

CHARMING

An upholstered
bedroom
is hushed
and settled.

You're cocooned from the rest
of the world. Generally, I just
glue the paper-backed fabric
onto the walls instead of
inserting extra padding, for a
crisper look. The repetition of
the pattern of the linen on the
headboard further puts you at
ease. There's a precedent to
using all one pattern in a room
that goes back to French Toile
de Jouy. Since we're not all still
wistful over that junior year
abroad in Provence, I generally
skip that blue-and-white
restricted motif for something
a little less exagéré.

Well, you certainly can't miss the charm here— especially with the abundance of gingham, which is irrefutably the zenith of c-h-a-r-m.

It's both humble and enchanting. I have forty thousand colorways of gingham in my design library, and I make every effort to use them all. Believe me, it absolutely can't fail, whether you're in a posh city penthouse or a rambling country cottage.

CHARMING

A wicker basket, a copper pot, a bamboo curtain rod—all of these elements come together to create an unabashedly charming room.

There's nothing saccharine here, just a creative mix of patterns, colors, and details that deliver joy with their unexpected whimsy and creativity. There's something very friendly about a bench at a table. An armless, backless picnic bench is fine if you need to suddenly flee from a charging bear while having a sandwich in a national park, but really, a bench should provide comfort. This is a job for upholstery. Adding a bench with a seat cushion and throw pillows is just the ticket for a super relaxed breakfast or lunch. This makes those meals so much more convivial and charming.

Chipper robin's-egg blue paint, open shelving, and polished oak countertops come together to create a warm, welcoming kitchen that bucks the trend of slabs of granite and stainless-steel appliances.

I'm rather nonplussed about cold, antiseptic kitchens and smitten with those that are warm and inviting.

A quintessential
element of charm
is the feeling that
a space is lived in.

If it feels like no one is home, there's no
charm. Nada. There are lots of details at
play in this room that provide the kind of
spirit that goes beyond just being
attractive—glistening nailhead trim, a
smattering of repurposed dining chairs,
antlers galore, a tiger throw pillow, even a
pumpkin lacquered ceiling. All of these
elements are kept in check by the
symmetry of it all. But do you want to
know the reason this room is so lived in?
The sofas can be converted into beds,
making it useful both day and night.

CHARMING

I'm the guy who always finds displays of fruit charming (even in the grocery store!).

Here is a piece of fruit on steriods. When a single pear is rendered in porcelain at such an enormous scale, it is divine.

When most people think of eating outside, they think of paper plates.

Shame on you! What are you afraid of? Haul the good stuff out and see your china and flatware in a whole new light when presented on a more rusticated table. And don't bother with the place mats—they'd look preposterous out here. You'll enjoy the imperfections of a reclaimed wood table just as much as you will that fresh air.

Layers add charm for one good reason.

You can't buy layering all at once; you have to build it piece by piece. The wall of books that anchors the bed, the paintings hung in front of the shelves, the mismatched bedside tables—they are all telling a story just oozing with personality. But know when to stop! There's a nasty rumor out there that a room is never done, and I flat-out disagree. There is most certainly a logical stopping point. So, take a step back with a glass of frosty Chablis in hand, and know when you've done enough. Or take two steps back and have a second glass of Chablis, at which point you're really done!

Styling a sideboard is all about a mix of scale and materials.

A plaster decorative urn takes a surprising spin with a Navajo basket and an edited stack of white books.

The primary goal is to see the big picture first and dig deeper to discover the series of smaller pictures within.

A powder room is not the most highly trafficked area in the home.

For that reason alone, it becomes a marvelous place to experiment with rare and interesting materials. The base of the sink is bamboo that was once the stand of an unexpected birdcage. The basin was crafted from an Indian copper bowl— installing it is as easy as asking your plumber to drill a hole in the bottom and there you go. In such a small room you can take enormous liberties and be forgiven if they don't all play out. Give them a try!

CHARMING

Why have just two guest towels when you can have a whole wall of them?

It's just as easy to buy three towel bars as it is to buy one, so creating this "ladder" is a snap, while collecting vintage guest towels is a treat. This joyful approach to a powder-room standard introduces an unexpectedly delightful moment and encourages us all to exercise our creativity.

Don't be tempted to hide the flaws of an imperfect space.

Take advantage of the quirky, existing materials. Here, I painted the brick white and brought visual interest to the walls and ceiling by adding textured plaster. I'd take these endearing materials any day of the week over smooth, perfect, nondescript sheetrock, the very definition of charmless.

The homespun American beauty of a patchwork quilt can be counted on to add color, pattern, and charm to any bedroom.

Layer on the patterns for a modern mix that's uniquely warm and welcoming. Despite its humble origins, this iconic textile has captured the hearts of generations of style mavens from Gloria Vanderbilt and Renzo Mongiardino to Raf Simons. I recently repurposed this quilt as a tablecloth and it transitioned flawlessly. Actually, I can't think of anything that's not "transitioning" these days, so #trending! Patterns cohabitate naturally if you select from a broad range. Too much geometric and you run the risk of an op-art meltdown. Too many botanical prints and garden-show fatigue sets in. But a combination of both yields satisfying and settled results that complement each other.

CHARMING

I'm rather smitten with the idea of a serve-yourself bar.

Call me lazy but I think it's a bore to refill someone else's glass all the time and a lot more
fun to have them do it themselves. They take care of the refills, and you take care of the empties.

The windswept hanging of these botanical prints adds a liberating lyricism to this dining room.

There's no adhering to a script, but they're not arranged in a completely random fashion either. Although they break out of the grid commonly used to display sets, each print still maintains equal spacing on at least one of its four sides with its neighbor. Not to be overlooked is the power of botanicals en masse. They can be purchased rather inexpensively and create such a major impact. Avoid any prints with rigid geometry (like architectural elevations), which insist you hang them in a more linear fashion.

Too many urban outdoor spaces suffer from being overly formulaic.

By exercising the power to add life and personality to a terrace, you'll discover just how charming they can be. There's plenty that makes this one so successful. Of course, landscape design by Miranda Brooks helps. The little reed-and-pole structure adds a bit of architecture without any fuss, extra pillows from inside connect the two spaces, and groupings of garden seats and planters are just more fun than one big cocktail table. Creating a sanctuary isn't so hard after all.

CHARMING

Extraordinarily versatile, wicker works just as well indoors as it does out.

By bringing this settee in from the garden, its charms are even more apparent. The unexpected treat of taking furniture or objects out of context allows you to explore their virtues in a wholly new manner. Conjure an image of a weathervane in a New York City apartment, and I think you get the picture.

The entry to this house was absolutely overwhelmed by its staircase.

To combat that visual strength and soften the blow, I had to create a charming resolution to balance this architectural force. A skirted table draws the eye down. The back wall is painted dark so it falls into deep shadow. The same printed linen that covers the other walls is used as a curtain. Here the charm offensive is in full effect.

COZY

Cozy is such a great word. I love saying it. Really, I feel more like singing it. And for me, cozy conjures up an immediate sense of, well, everything that you want in a home. Of all the chapters in this book, cozy is the most important and in a way the culmination of all the other attributes that we've covered. It's the end result of all of our efforts.

When things feel like they are in their place—and of their place—that's when a room is cozy. It's comforting to be in a cozy room because everything seems settled, with nothing superfluous or unresolved. It's what permits you to sink in and be at ease in your own environment. In my mind, every room can and should be cozy. Now, don't get cozy confused with quaint or cute, casual or cottage. This type of cozy is far more elegant, thoughtful, and astute than that.

Furniture groupings are an important way to create this sense, by breaking large rooms down into conversational hubs. Picking furniture of the right scale for the space is essential as well. Ever felt like you were sitting on a throne or perching on a thimble? Neither of those scenarios makes you feel cozy. There's also the opportunity to create cozy spaces in often overlooked places like the bathroom, which doesn't necessarily have to be covered wall to wall in slabs of marble. I feel the same way about the kitchen, which has been taken over by sterile mixes of stainless steel and cold stone, when it used to be the coziest place in the house. Why not put some heart back into what once was the hearth?

Cozy is the human quality in a room, and that's what connects us and makes us feel at home. Welcome to cozy. Thank you; you're welcome.

Cozy can be glamorous.

For all of its nailheads and bouillon fringe, this room is really quite settling because of its monochromatic palette of grays. By picking one color for the walls, carpet, and upholstery, the room has the power to envelop. And it doesn't have to be gray—just choose your favorite color and explore its spectrum.

Big rooms need small moments.

Adding a panel of contrasting cloth to the base of these theatrically scaled white curtains lowered the sight-line and created a wraparound effect. The khaki color helps us see the silhouettes of the furniture and embraces the intimate grouping of upholstery.

Time to grab your tape measure.

Creating a space you want to sink into isn't just about the furniture you pick. Equally important is how the furniture is arranged, and there are a few measurement rules that I live by. The edge of the coffee table should be seventeen inches from the sofa—it's close enough to reach for a drink but far away enough to easily walk around. The chairs in frame facing the sofa should be about half that distance from the table since it can be easily be moved out when pressed into service. Flanking chairs are perfect at twenty-one inches from the table, because they usually have their own side tables. If you play by the numbers, you really can't go wrong.

When decorating a bedroom, start at the top.

The addition of a decorative detail on the ceiling, such as wallpaper, reeding, or an unexpected paint color, brings interest to the part of the room you notice the most when in bed.

COZY

Tonality is a big part of the coziness of this library.

It's not playing into those typical library preconceptions that it must be red, brown, or paneled. Instead it's awash in golden shades, all staying in the same family. Even the hand-painted, faux bois bookcases pick up on this palette, which calms the space with its consistency and warmth. While we're on the subject of library preconceptions . . . the nailhead trim applied to the walls alludes to a paneled room but renders it with completely unexpected materials that are both original and economical.

I do obsess about bedside lamps, and as fantastically alluring as a big tabletop lamp on a bedside table can be, they take up way too much room.

With a wall-mounted, swing-arm lamp you can bring it closer or push it away without getting out of bed. That way you can lull yourself to sleep and just reach out when you need to shut off the light. Anything you have to reach too far or roll over for is not worth it (your mate included).

Cozy doesn't have to be casual.

People can misconceive cozy as cottagey. This urban space is incredibly sophisticated yet keeps things relaxed with the soft shapes of the upholstered furnishings. Not all sofas are designed to be flush to the wall. Some reach out with their arms and wrap right around you. The accentuated curve of the arm in the foreground keeps the eye circulating, traveling from the perimeter back to the round ottoman, another welcoming piece in this refined room.

COZY

Big, bold, brassy moves like colorful curtains and sofa should be tempered with delicacy. Fragile blossoming branches soften the edges in powerful spaces.

Go ahead and say it: Purple. Purple, purple, purple!

Saturated colors, especially on walls and trim, immerse you in a room
and create spaces that envelope you like a comfortable sweater.

It's absolutely natural to get cabin fever in winter.

To satisfy those outdoor longings when the temperature drops, turn a loggia into a multi-seasonal escape. Instead of staring out the window at a leaf-strewn porch, leave a few pieces of furniture in a semi-covered space and "winterize" it with the addition of some warm blankets and an outdoor carpet. This room is defined by no more than cords of wood stacked between columns to create a wind block, with a window cleverly inserted to retain the view. Who wouldn't want to venture out there for a little break during family holiday celebrations?

COZY

There's a secret about me that isn't so secret.

I live and breathe for canopied beds, and I consider this version one of my greatest triumphs. What's really working here is that the interior of the bed is warm while the room itself is much cooler. Albert Hadley, the dean of American decorating, once told me that bedrooms are meant to be a bit "frosty." But the takeaway here is that he was talking about the bedroom, not the bed itself. The orange and ivory quilt at the foot of the bed, the deep teal headboard, and the parchment-colored hangings create a warm palette that draws you in and under the covers.

Every type of chair has a specific purpose, and generally their names hint at what they're supposed to do.

This is a contiguous wing chair, a riff on a classic wing chair. It still has the clean, architectural lines you might expect, but it is a bit more contemporary. The back is rigid with a defined arc, yet the seat is cozy enough to lean back into and relax. Great for reading and relaxing by a fireplace—just be sure you have a book, a cup of coffee, a tartan lap robe, and your beloved pet before you settle in.

COZY

There's no rule that says bookcases have to be pushed up against the wall.
They're portable and can land just about anywhere. Here, they act as semitransparent room dividers sectioning this library into two cozier spaces. An added bonus—you can now admire both the spines and the wildly beautiful paper edges that lend a wonderful rhythm all their own.

COZY

I'm more for
breaking
decorating
rules than
setting them.
But the one I do live by is
that if you use a pattern at
the window, you must see it
somewhere else in the
room. If not, your eye will
go to the print of the
curtain and get stuck there.
The repetition of pattern
diffuses impact and unifies
its success, allowing you to
remember the beauty of
the room, not just curtains.

Cozy conveys snug.

That said, a fourteen-foot sofa that fills an entire wall certainly delivers. (Fun fact: the largest sofa I've ever done was 148 feet. Just think about that!) What makes it even more inviting is the overstuffed cushions. I prefer six to eight inches of depth, when standard issue is really only a measly three or four inches. One of my biggest tricks is to have new plumper cushions made for existing sofas to achieve the same look with less expense than fabricating an entirely custom piece.

COZY

COZY

Don't think
of it as just a
bathroom!
It should
be treated
like any other
furnished
room.
When there's extra space, add
a sofa or a chair and all of
sudden you've got a sanctuary
where you can plunk down
in your fluffy white robe and
no one will bother you.

When exploring the cozy comforts of a canopy bed, you can always embrace the effect incrementally.

When my clients are resistant, I'll start with just the structure of a tester bed. From there, I'll layer in a roof and a back panel before going for the full canopy with sides. Nothing makes for a better night's sleep than a roof over your head.

In my book, a slipper chair and a settee are the two "s" words that are never mentioned enough.

In a room with several groupings of furniture, it's important to scale one down. A sofa in frame keeps things lean and elegant, while the armless chair doesn't hold its guest captive like a club chair would. Nestle them up to a slim tea table, and now you've got a place for a civilized conversation.

To create intimacy in a room of this scale, details cannot be overlooked.

While it may seem that bold gestures are needed, instead it's the layering of thoughtful touches that make one want to stay a little longer. The window seat covered in a nutmeg cashmere begs to be caressed, the tangerine banding on the curtain pulls the eye to the window, and the pair of chairs spiffed up with alternating nailheads invite you to stay awhile.

How can we take something not built for comfort and refresh it in a way that seems more contemporary?

No one was ever going to sit in this rigid early nineteenth-century American bench until we added a straightforward, two-inch box-cushion Greek mattress with a playful contrast stitch. That plus a few pillows was all it took to transform this family albatross. Oops, I meant heirloom.

COZY

First impressions really do mean the most.

When it comes to welcoming guests into your home, be sure to make them feel cozy from the get-go. This entry creates an intimate world filled with rich colors and tactile materials. A printed cloth we had embroidered and bobbed on a rod creates the perfect backdrop for carefully curated objects that tell the story of those who live here.

A reading nook delivers a clear message to relax and stay awhile.

With a sofa tucked back into a recess of books, there's a sense that you're out of the traffic flow of the room. It feels protected, safe, and cozy, especially with details such as the sofa back that scoops down to make a shelf of books more accessible. In this case, we took back the space from an unnecessary closet to fashion a place far more functional.

I don't think anyone has ever met a mantel that isn't tempting to dress.

It's the no-brainer of decorating. But where to start? I like to play with scale and proportion and constantly change mine up, adding vases, cut glass—really, anything pretty or meaningful. The only mistake to be made is overdecorating. Just steer clear of that four-foot candelabra, and remember the roaring fire is already making the big statement; you're just embellishing it.

COZY

COZY

It's never a surprise when a client requests a built-in banquette or window seat.

Everyone wants one, but in this mudroom it really was the perfect solution, providing both under-seat storage and a place to take off shoes. I like to keep them at a shallow perching level—I find seventeen to nineteen inches to be the best height, with twenty-one inches as the max. Ask and you shall receive.

Although a corona may look fancy, one can be put together with only four pieces of lumber and a hammer.

For a child's room, it creates a wonderful sense of security and containment mixed with a splash of camping tent appeal. To keep things simple, I chose an unlined cotton with an easy box pleat that can be assembled with some Velcro or a staple gun. Remember to leave a buttonhole above the headboard to include a lamp for bedtime stories and homework.

ACKNOWLEDGMENTS

It's often assumed that authors craft their own books, but truth be told, I've always worked in tandem with great writers: Jacqueline Terrebonne has a long history within the design industry and with me, and I'm thrilled she could bring her expert insight to this book and enthusiastically enhance its unique, modern approach to how we share our stories and knowledge. I thank Rizzoli and publisher Charles Miers for believing in *Everyday Decorating* with the same conviction as *Design Basics*, written almost sixteen years ago. To Doug Turshen and Steve Turner, who can read my shorthand better than any other art directors (this is our fourth collaboration!). To Andrea Danese, who inherited this book and made it her own through focused and reassuring edits (alas, I'm not easy to please). To the photographers and agents whom (I hope) are well represented in these pages and who provided the highest quality images from recent and archival projects (no simple task). To Levi Blasdel, who is my assistant and who has a very full plate yet is somehow able to stay focused on the tasks at hand (and still tirelessly believes in me and the opportunities ahead).

Providing expert advice and beautifully crafted products have always been a hallmark of my work. My growing list of manufacturing partners understands that we're only as good as what we deliver. My thanks to Product Lounge, my agents for helping me build a strong stable of partners such as Chesneys, de Gournay, Henredon, The Lacquer Company, Mirth Studio, and Stark Carpet. I am proudest of my partnerships and our shared goals to design, build, sell, and distribute products that consumers and clients covet and cherish.

GLORIA NATALIE BILHUBER (1929–2018) instilled in me a powerful sense of place and the importance of home. I grew up with three brothers. By the time I was sixteen, we had lived in five houses in four states and two countries, but thanks to our mother, we were all encouraged to create a room to call our own.

Every day I design, create, build, curate, and decorate beautiful rooms.

I sketch to scale (which is not as difficult as it sounds) and build color boards based on gardens, fashion, and modern society. Always surround yourself with the inspirations, images, and materials that you love or want to nurture, improve, and cultivate.

PHOTO CREDITS

William Abranowicz: 122, 123, 142, 167, 171, 194, 196–197, 205, 235, 248

Jean Allsopp: 90

Fernando Bengoechea: 18–19, 62, 106–107, 110, 114, 147, 249, 253

Pascal Chevallier: 55, 116–117

Roger Davies: 191, 234

Scott Frances: 176–177

Don Freeman: 26, 88–89, 146, 160, 210, 219, 224–225

Kari Haavisto: 232–233

Henredon: 12, 38, 39, 44–45, 64–65, 74–75, 94, 108–109, 115, 179, 182–183, 184, 208, 255

Lizzie Himmel: 158–159

Thibault Jeanson: 92, 93

Thomas Loof: 4, 76, 77, 82–83, 230, 231, back cover

Peter Margonelli: 13, 14–15, 32–33, 47, 78–79, 105, 111, 126, 137, 141, 143, 154–155, 157, 166, 170, 180, 198, 199, 202–203, 204, 215, 221, 240–241, 244–245

Keith Scott Morton: 195, 206–207, 226, 228–229

Peter Murdock: 28–29, 34, 35, 46, 102–103, 128, 130–131, 144–145, 150, 152, 153, 156, 242, 252

One Kings Lane: 36–37, 52–53, 54, 70–71, 72, 73, 98–99, 104, 118, 119, 127, 136, 151, 172–173, 192–193, 201, 211, 212–213, 214, 218, 250–251

Eric Piasecki: 175, 178, 181, 227

Richard Powers: 56–57, 60–61, 148–149, 168–169, 186–187, front and back endpapers

Kelly Taub: 6

Chi Chi Ubina: 81, 85, 200, 238, 239

Simon Upton: 16, 20–21, 22–23, 30, 43, 50, 51, 58–59, 80, 84, 91, 129, 134–135, 246

Peter Vanderwarker: 190

William Waldron: 9, 24–25, 40–41, 48–49, 100–101, 112–113, 138–139, 163, 165, 174, 209, 215, 236–237

Bjorn Wallander: 2, 10–11, 95, 97, 120–121, 133, 140, 185, 216–217, front cover

Jillian Wass: 17, 27, 31, 63, 66, 67, 69, 86, 87, 124–125, 161, 189, 223, 243, 247

First published in the United States of American in 2019
By Rizzoli International Publications, Inc.
300 Park Avenue South
New York, NY 10010
www.rizzoliusa.com

Designed by Doug Turshen with Steve Turner

ISBN-13: 978-0-8478-6634-2

Library of Congress Control Number: 2018965335

2019 2020 2021 2022 / 10 9 8 7 6 5 4 3 2 1

Distributed in the U.S. trade by Random House, New York

Printed in China

JEFFREY BILHUBER is the founder and principal designer of Bilhuber & Associates. His work has been published in more than two hundred books and in every major design magazine in the United States and abroad. He is a regular on the AD100 and *Elle Decor* A-List. He has collaborated on an extensive list of product lines, including those with Stark Carpet, de Gournay, Henredon, The Lacquer Company, Elson & Company, Chesneys, and Mirth Studio. Most recently he partnered with The Perfect Room, a curated digital marketplace. He is the recipient of the 2019 Albert Hadley Lifetime Achievement Award from New York School of Interior Design. *Everyday Decorating* is his fifth book with Rizzoli.

JACQUELINE TERREBONNE serves as *Galerie*'s editor in chief, after originally joining the team in the role of design editor in 2016. Her varied artistic interests and deep sense of curiosity informs the diverse and eclectic mix of design, fashion, and visual arts in every issue of the magazine. Prior to her work at *Galerie*, Terrebonne held positions at *Architectural Digest*, *Gourmet*, and *Martha Stewart Living*. She is also a member of BAFTA and the James Beard Foundation.